THE NEW ABC

That will positively help to change

Your life for the better

And help make

**EVERYTHING IN LIFE POSSIBLE AND
NOTHING IMPOSSIBLE**

Jill Divine

ISBN: 978-1-4457-8529-5

Other published books by Jill Divine

Poetry Emotion ISBN: 978-1-4452-3529-5

Published by Divinelady

Anjoy – God's Gifts ISBN: 1413764657

Published by PublishAmerica (Sci-fi)

The Bears ISBN: 1-4241-0307-X

Published by PublishAmerica (Sci-fi)

Miles Smiles ISBN: 978-1-4092-5052-4

Published by www.lulu.com (Children 4 – 6 years)

The Alien Who Came To Tea ISBN: 978-1-4092-8010-1

Published by www.lulu.com (Children 6 – 8 years)

More about Jill Divine and her writing can be seen on her website
www.divinelady.co.uk

First printing by Lulu.com

British Library Cataloguing in Publication Data

A Record of this Publication is available from the British Library

Published by Divinelady

Front cover, © illustrated by Jill Divine

To David, my wonderful son, who has been a positive help and encouragement in all of my life and especially with my writing.

And, to all of my friends who have started me on my own positive journey.

CONTENTS

Introduction

The Divine Lady and Her Mexican Wave of Smiles.

POSITIVE©

Positive. Such a wonderful word for a start.

Once you become it, you open your heart.

Start by having a positive thought every day

In everything you do and whatever you say.

Try just saying the word, see how you feel.

It doesn't cost anything, it's no big deal.

Very important though if you want to survive.

Energizing your thoughts to feel positively alive.

INTRODUCTION

The Divine Lady and Her Mexican Wave of Smiles

Five years ago Jill Divine was surrounded by negative energy, chronically disabled with rheumatoid arthritis and in an unhappy marriage, she was slowly suffocating. In her own words she existed rather than felt alive. Thankfully her belief in angels kept a tiny positive spark inside her alive that led her to meditation. During meditation she visualized an amazing story that continued throughout her meditations. Suddenly her positive spark had ignited and she was now inspired to write that story down.

Up until then she had no interest in writing and didn't even know how to write, in fact she'd rather read than write. The words flowed and her hand had difficulty keeping up with her mind. Since then the inspiration has not stopped and she continues to write. Through her love of writing, she hopes to inspire more people to become positive and bring love and light into the world.

Jill's first published book, Anjoy – God's Gifts, was her FIRST step to help foster world peace. This book depicts a planet set in the future where positive energy disappears and negativity takes control, and shows what could happen to our planet if we let this happen. This received excellent reviews from Uri Geller and USA celebrity reporter Anne Brodie.

However on 15th December 2005 Jill took her next step and **GIANT** leap forward to help make our universe a happier, smiling, and positive place to live in when she appeared on American television on The Happiness Show (White Plains, New York, cable 76 access) and started her **MEXICAN WAVE OF SMILES.**

She told listeners how energy worked and how if each and everyone of us could become more positive in everything that we do and say we may help to foster world peace, and that a smile was the quickest and easiest way to raise the positive energy. She asked everyone to take her smile and hoped that viewers would spread it to others so that it would act like a Mexican wave, and if spread far enough, could help raise the positive energy all around the universe. If more people were positive they would be more inclined to, (metaphorically speaking of course), "love thy neighbour" and less inclined to argue or fight, and ultimately start that war. Peace in our time would be a reality and not just a dream.

She is pleased to say that this Mexican wave of smiles spread as far as Australia and New Zealand and that it is still rippling in England.

If you would like to see this ten minute piece of film you can watch it on the internet on http://thehappinessshow.com show number 125.

NOW READ ON TO DISCOVER HOW TO BRING POSITIVE ENERGY INTO YOUR LIFE AND HOW TO HELP MAKE EVERYTHING POSSIBLE AND NOTHING IMPOSSIBLE.

CHAPTER ONE

Back to School

The ABC is the first lesson everyone is taught when they start school. Once you've mastered this, then you progress to reading and of course once you can read then the world is your oyster. You can now fill your head with knowledge and start to lead your own life.

But now we must all go back to school and learn our **Positive Energy ABC**. Once we have learnt this then everything in life becomes possible, and nothing becomes impossible.

If each and everyone of us could learn how to follow the **Positive Energy ABC** and keep it in our lives in everything we do and say, then not only will we feel wonderful, but it will also raise the positive energy in the world and make our universe a positively wonderful place to live in, so peace in our time may become possible and not just a dream.

NOT POSSIBLE?

If you're thinking this, then read on, because already you've only got as far as the **A** in the **Positive Energy ABC**. You've acted positive by buying this book because you want to bring positive energy into your lives, but you haven't cast off all your negative energy, because you don't truly believe that everything is possible. You are still telling yourself it is impossible.

So, whether you believe or not, then turn over and take your seat for the first day at the **Positive Energy** school. Here we will learn how:-

EVERYTHING IS POSSIBLE
AND NOTHING IS IMPOSSIBLE.

CHAPTER 2
Positive Energy School

Here is your new **Positive Energy ABC.** From now on this is just as important as the ABC you learnt at school.

> **A** is for **ACT** POSITIVE
>
> **B** is for **BELIEVE** POSITIVE
>
> **C** is for **CAST** OFF NEGATIVITY

It sounds so easy, doesn't it? Many of us I am pleased to say do **Act** positive, but then so many of us fall at the wayside because we don't carry on and **Believe** positive. If we **Believed** positively in everything we did and said, then **Casting** off negative energy would be so much easier. The world would be your oyster, because having learnt your **Positive Energy ABC,** you would now know that everything in life is possible and nothing is impossible.

Over the following pages I will show you many ways how to, not just learn to use the **Positive Energy ABC,** but also how to keep it in your lives in everything you do and say.

CHAPTER THREE

How to See and Feel Energy

Having got this far and learnt the basic **Positive Energy ABC**, now let me tell you how you can see and feel both positive and negative energies so that you can understand your new **ABC** a little better.

POSITIVE ENERGY ATTRACTS
NEGATIVE ENERGY REPELS

Many people work and it is here that the different energies we give out with our thoughts, words, and actions, can make you love or hate your job. Let me take you in to two different offices, the first one is a joy to work in, whereas the second office will make you sad or fill you with rage.

If you constantly work in the second office, then I suggest you ask for a transfer before you completely suffocate, or explode!

(These examples are also experienced in everything you do in life, even if you don't go out to work. Once you've visualized walking into both of these offices, you will see what I mean).

OFFICE ONE – POSITIVE ENERGY ATTRACTS

Let's walk into the first office. As we open the door you can instantly feel the positive energy in the room. The air feels wonderful, it's like being by the sea and you're getting a whiff of fresh air. In this office people are laughing, joking, perhaps sharing good news, and also smiling. Because they feel so positive, their mind, body, and souls are working positively well. Everything that they do, or say today, will work really well.

Communications with people over the telephone will be easier because the other person will feel and respond positively to their positive energy. Any decisions that were previously causing problems will now be solved. Positive people can always find a way to the solution.

When you are positive:-

EVERYTHING IS POSSIBLE

NOTHING IS IMPOSSIBLE

More importantly if you work in this office when you leave it, you take this positive energy away with you. You send it out to the people you meet going home. Even by simply smiling at them. They may have had a hard day, but your positive smile will be welcomed.

When you arrive home, you carry on sharing this positive energy with your family. You've brought that whiff of fresh air home with you. Even if you are tired and need to relax before you start making tea, or playing with the children, others will understand because they are in a positive mood, so will leave you to relax.

(You will understand this last sentence better after you've unfortunately left the next office).

OFFICE TWO – NEGATIVE ENERGY REPELS

Fasten your seatbelts because you're now in for a bumpy ride! You are opening the door to the second office.

As soon as you open this door the energy hits you and you instinctively want to leave. ***You can cut the atmosphere with a knife.*** The air feels thick and suffocating. This room feels as if you are walking into thick black smoke, you can barely breathe because in this office everyone is moaning, groaning, arguing, or even shouting at each other.

How many times have you walked into this office? Your colleagues' faces are frowning or full of woe and someone says something as simple as this:-

"I've had a terrible morning, the tube was full."

"It's pouring with rain. This weather is awful."

"I've got a sore throat; I think I've got a cold coming."

Because negative energy repels and you don't want that energy, you want to give it straight back. So you will find yourself joining in with their woes and saying:-

"I got soaked in the rain too and now I've got a sore throat."

All it takes is something as simple as moaning about how you feel and you will soon find the whole office sharing your symptoms and feeling too bad to work positively that day. The work will pile up as you struggle to work in this negative energy.

Even worse if someone is shouting and sends that anger to you, then you will find yourself instantly shouting or arguing back. If you have to work in this energy all day then all thoughts become difficult. Nothing seems to go right. In fact the day goes from bad to worse. Remember the energy in this office is like sitting in thick smoke, so you are unable to make any rational or even positive decisions, because your brain is being suffocated.

You will spend the day trying to give this negative energy back, because you don't like how it feels.

IT REPELS YOU!

Now, thankfully it's time to go home. But because you are feeling so low and fed up, you still continue to give out this negative energy to everyone you meet. Oh, and of course all traffic lights will be on stop. The tube will be late or full. Everything will seem to be against you reaching home to relax.

WHY?

Because in your negative mood you are **expecting** all of this to happen, and having sent that energy out, then of course that's what will happen. When you expect something to happen, it does!

At last we reach home, and all you want to do is chill out, but the children or partner are anxiously waiting to greet you. What do you do?

REPEL them of course, by shouting, moaning, or arguing with them.

Now what happens?

They've received your negative energy and so they give it back to you.

Boy, are you feeling bad right now!

I'm sure you'd rather be working in the other office. Wouldn't you?

So, if you can't ask for a transfer, then let's deal with your office and change the energy in it.

HOW TO CAST OFF NEGATIVE ENERGY FROM OFFICE TWO

Don't worry; this becomes easier the more times you do it.

'**C**' is the hardest letter of your **Positive Energy ABC** to learn and get past, but once you do, the world becomes your oyster and a much more enjoyable place to live in.

Having been in that office the previous day, we are now going to start the morning in a different energy. As soon as you wake up you start by telling yourself:-

"It's a **wonderful** day, and it **will** be wonderful."

"You **expect** everything to go **positively** well."

BELIEVE those words. No negative thoughts, such as:-

"What a **terrible** morning. The weather's **awful**."

"I'm **not** looking forward to today. I'm sure it will be a **bad** one."

Instead tell yourself:-

"It **IS** going to be a good day and so what if it's raining – the ducks will like it!"

(Or words to that effect, but I hope you get my meaning).

Now when you walk into your office you continue telling yourself that everything will be positively wonderful and you are not going to take anyone's negative energy. It repels you. **Believe** in those words, and keep on **Believing** in them.

As you enter, those who are in a bad, or just fed up, but in negative moods, will notice your positive energy. Because positive energy attracts they will see how you feel, and want to take some of that energy.

REMEMBER YOU ARE NOT GOING TO TAKE ANY OF THEIRS THOUGH!

If they are moaning, or arguing, then you don't join in. Instead, share your positive energy with them. Work and speak in a positive manner and most importantly keep on smiling. They will soon take some of that energy and join in. Gradually the energy in your office will change. As the positive energy rises, the air becomes fresher and everyone finds how much easier and more enjoyable it is to think and make decisions now that thick smoke has gone. They become even more positive in everything they do and say.

Soon your office becomes like the first one we visited. Now there's no need to ask for that transfer, because you've done something positive about it.

But this will only happen if you've **Cast** off all negativity and **Believe** positively in everything you do and say.

If not, I'm afraid you will continue to work in that suffocating negative office.

CHAPTER FOUR

How to Use Your Positive Energy ABC

I am now going to show you how by using your words and thoughts that others can see and feel your energy.

I am going to use a job interview as an example because it is something that makes many people nervous and you can see how your thoughts could affect what happens on the big day!

You've **Acted** positive in making the decision to go for that job. Having done this, many people (both men and women), will have decided what they are going to wear for that interview so that they look their best. Yet, having decided you look positively wonderful in that outfit, on the day of the interview, or perhaps the night before, you suddenly decide to change something.

WHY?

Very simply, because you're not **Believing** how good you look. Something as simple as that tiny thought will have lowered your positive energy because you don't believe you will look good enough to get the position.

You now start to panic as you look for something else to wear, but none of your clothes look right on you today so gets rejected one by one. If this happens on the day of the interview then whilst your mind is panicking it is allowing a tiny seed of doubt to grow and other negative thoughts now enter your mind.

"What if the tube is late?"

"What if the car won't start?"

"What if I can't answer their questions?"

So many, 'What ifs?' and negative thoughts from that one tiny negative seed.

All seeds grow, and, if weeds, will spread. Think of negative energy as a weed, and by spreading it with your thoughts you are transferring that seed to other people's energy, and by doing so allowing them to think negative thoughts about you too.

When you get to the interview, if you've allowed any one of these tiny negative seeds to enter your mind, then others will notice it. The interviewers will notice it!

"I liked that person, **but there was something I just couldn't quite put my finger on why they weren't good enough for this position.**"

Energy is always seen and felt. They felt your negative energy. Your previous thoughts had already told them that you weren't quite good enough for this position, simply because you didn't **Believe** in yourself.

By changing everything that you say and do to:

"I look **good**."

"The tube **will** be on time."

"The car **will** start."

"I **can** answer all their questions **positively**, because I am the **best** person for that job."

You will feel really positive, and they will see and feel this, because positive people shine and it is always noticed. Positive people are confident in everything they do and say and will always succeed. They know everything is possible and nothing is impossible.

And, why do positive people succeed? Because they:-

Believe in themselves.

Believe in their thoughts.

Believe in their actions.

They've now **Cast** off all negative energy.

Having **Cast** off all negative energy, we now have to be very careful that we don't take other people's negative energy.

It can be very easily and simply done, and the person giving you this negative energy may be your friend who doesn't even realize what they've done, because they think they are being kind and helping you!

For example, this position you've **Acted** positive about, is something which is very different to what you would normally do. You are confident that you can do this work and so **Act** positive and apply for the position and **Believe** you will get it.

Your friend however, may not be so confident, and will try to push their negative thoughts onto you so that you change your mind about it.

They don't have your confidence, and in fact can't get further than **A** in the **Positive Energy ABC.**

"Why are you trying for that job? I'm sure you won't like it. You won't be any good at it. Why don't you stay where you are?"

They think they are helping you, but in fact they are actually sending negative thoughts out, and unless you carry on **Believing** in yourself and are positive that you can do this job, then you won't be able to **Cast** off the negative energy that they are sending to you.

DON'T take their negative energy!

Remember you are **POSITIVE** about what you want to do.

CHAPTER FIVE

Applying Your Positive Energy ABC to Daily Life

Your new **Positive Energy ABC** can be used for everything you do in life. Whether you want to stop smoking, lose weight, cut down on your drinking, or change your life for the better in any other way, use your **Positive Energy ABC** and make sure you follow it.

Having made the decision to change your life you've:-

ACTED positive

Now you must positively BELIEVE

Positively **BELIEVE** in how you are going to do it and think positively in what you say.

To stop smoking or to lose weight are on the top of the list for many people who wish to change their lives for the better. I have therefore used these two examples to show why you may have previously failed, and how you can now succeed simply by changing your thoughts and stopping those previous negative seeds that you may have allowed to grow and fill you with negative energy.

STOP SMOKING

If someone has told you that you **MUST** give up smoking then it is not your decision, but theirs, and it will make it harder for you to **Believe** in yourself and give up smoking.

You will find it a lot easier to stop smoking if you have made the decision yourself. Having **Acted** positively, you must now decide how **YOU** are going to do it. This is your decision no one else's! Think positively about it. You may decide to stop smoking straightaway, or cut down. Perhaps use patches? Whatever your decision, **Believe** it will work. No words such as:-

IF I can cut down today.

Or, I **HOPE** these patches will work.

Or, **THE HARDEST** part will be having a drink and not smoking.

You've already told yourself you don't **Believe** you can give up, so of course if won't be long before you'll fail and start smoking again. Think about what you are saying and how powerful the mind is. It listens to those negative words and stops you from giving up. Take control of your mind and change those words to positive ones

Change all of these words to:-

>   I **WILL** cut down on my cigarettes today;
>
>   I **EXPECT** to **SUCCEED** in cutting down today.
>
>   These patches **WILL** work, I **EXPECT** them to **SUCCEED.**
>
>   I **KNOW** I can drink and not want a cigarette.

Once you start positively **Believing** in yourself, then giving up smoking becomes easier, because now you've **CAST** off all negative thoughts about failing. You know you can **SUCCEED.**

>   **IN FACT, YOU POSITIVELY EXPECT TO SUCCEED!**

DIETING

Again, as with stopping smoking, you have to want to lose weight. It is your decision, not someone else's. Once **you've** made the decision to lose weight you will have **Acted** positive. Now, as in smoking, you have to **Believe** in how you are going to lose weight.

It may be a low fat diet, cutting carbs, or joining a weight watching group. The decision is yours, and once again yours alone, but having decided on how you will lose weight, then **POSITIVELY BELIEVE** in it. The pounds will fall off you. Do not send negative words to your mind, such as:-

IF I can get through today without eating any biscuits.

The evening's the **HARDEST**, because I get so hungry.

Take control of your mind so that it knows you **Believe** in yourself and you are going to **SUCCEED** in losing weight. Try changing those words to:

I **WILL** get through today without eating any biscuits.

I **EXPECT** to do it without any problems.

I **WILL** get through the evening because I will be **POSITIVELY** enjoying myself doing other things, and I **POSITIVELY EXPECT TO SUCCEED.**

When you continue to **Act** positive and **Believe** in everything you do and say, you will find that you don't think of any cravings you may have. You only had those because you were putting those previous negative words into your mind and telling yourself that you needed those things. Now, as well as telling yourself that you don't need it, you are also positively telling yourself that you **EXPECT TO SUCCEED.**

If you positively expect something and **BELIEVE** in it. Then it **WILL** happen.

YOU WILL HAVE CAST OFF ALL NEGATIVE ENERGY.

However, as before with the job interview and learning to **Cast** off that friend's negative energy. Now, you must also remember not to take anyone else's negative views. Ignore those who say:-

"Oh, you've given up smoking before. It won't be long before you start again."

AND

"Go on, have a fag. You know you really want one."

OR

"What's the point of dieting? You'll only put the weight back on."

AND

"Forget about your diet. Men like chubby women/women like chubby men." (Perhaps they do, but remember you have made the decision to lose weight for yourself not to please others).

They are trying to stop you from losing weight because they haven't got your positive energy and also don't **Believe** in themselves so they will always fail at everything they attempt in life and encourage you to fail too!

However you do **Believe** in yourself and what's more you now know how to **Cast** off their negative energy.

So make sure you do and you will **SUCCEED** because you:-

EXPECT TO SUCCEED!

CHAPTER SIX

Loving Yourself

Having read this far and understood how your new **Positive Energy ABC** works, some of you may still be finding it difficult to practise and get past **A** or **B,** and failing at everything you want to do. The reason for this is simply because you don't love yourself.

I can hear some of you gasping with shock right now. Love myself? Is she mad? You don't love yourself! Well, not only it is alright to love yourself, but you should love yourself. Unless you start within by loving yourself, and knowing what a beautiful, wonderful, loving person you are, then it is harder to be positive about everything else in your life.

Once you love yourself you will feel positively good about anything. Love comes from within us and once we love ourselves and what we are, then we are able to share this love and send it out to others. You will positively shine at everything.

The reason so many people can't love themselves, or don't think it is right to love themselves, may be because of something that has happened in their past that has left them feeling unworthy, useless, and insecure about everything they do in life.

If you still have pain in your heart, soul, and mind, where others have hurt you in the past, now you must **Cast** off their negative energy. Because negative energy repels it makes you feel bad and unless you can **Cast** it off you will always have feelings of worthlessness, inadequacies, and repulsion about yourself. You will also attract this energy in every partner you meet in life, because you think you are second best and do not deserve the best.

This is why so many people in life end up with the same type of partner every time they start a new relationship. Initially this person seems wonderful, but as they have the same negative energy as all the other partners, eventually they will try to control you in one way or another. Control is a negative energy and so more negative energy sticks to you and you end up giving it out in one form or another, but mostly to yourself by feeling unworthy.

Let's untrap the mind and rid it of any past negative energy that has stopped you feeling beautiful and the best, and more importantly from attracting the best in life, whether in a relationship, job, or friends.

After reading the next chapter you will see that you don't have to feel, or accept, second best anymore.

CHAPTER SEVEN

Freeing the Butterfly

We are going to let yourself and everyone else see that beautiful butterfly that is inside your soul. Everyone has one, but yours has become stuck because of the negative energy you have received in the past and has turned it into a chrysalis. Now is the time to unzip it and release it for the whole world to see.

First, start by looking at yourself in the mirror. If you are unable to – because many people who don't love themselves – can't do this. Then buy a small lipstick mirror so that you can only see your lips. This is all we need to see.

If you are able to look into a full length mirror, but still feel a little uncomfortable doing so, think of yourself as a chrysalis. You are completely encased in a shell and zipped up the middle. All you can see are your lips.

Now you are going to smile. Then frown. Feel the difference in energy in your body. A frown lowers your energy and your whole body droops and you feel sad and lethargic. Whereas a smile lifts your face and your energy. It's attractive, so that's what others are seeing, but today this smile is just for you.

Tell yourself this smile is only for you and take its loving, positive energy down to your heart and keep it there. Now tell yourself you are beautiful and you **DESERVE** to be loved.

Because you are not used to loving yourself or thinking you are beautiful, and most importantly, deserve to be loved, then this may be one of the hardest things you have ever done –

SMILING AT YOURSELF AND TELLING YOURSELF YOU DESERVE TO BE LOVED!

Once you can do this simple exercise comfortably, increase that smile by taking it and giving it to yourself twice a day. Take its loving, positive energy down to your heart and soul and also remember to tell yourself that you are beautiful and loved.

It soon becomes easier as the loving positive energy increases inside you. Your positive flame, which was probably on pilot light, will now increase into a bigger flame. As it fills your positive energy you now start to realize how beautiful and lovely you truly are.

THE CHRYSALIS IS AWAKENING AND THE BUTTERFLY IS GETTING READY TO FLUTTER OUT AND SHOW EVERYONE YOUR TRUE BEAUTY.

When you have done this enough times and you truly realize how beautiful you are that butterfly will fly out. It doesn't matter what your physical body looks like, because all that people will see is your beautiful smile sending out its warm loving positive energy and also your beautiful soul which is no longer trapped, but free. You will shine with beauty.

Remember:-

POSITIVE PEOPLE SHINE

POSITIVE ENERGY ATTRACTS

OTHERS FEEL AND SEE THAT SHINE

Most importantly of all you now know you are not just **TRULY BEAUTIFUL,** but you are also **LOVED!**

CHAPTER EIGHT

Revision

The following chapters will show more examples of how energy works so that you can continue to understand how important your **Positive Energy ABC** is, and how your life will change for the better if you use it in everything that you say and do, and also how this positive energy when shared, may help to change our world positively for the better.

Having learnt how energy works, please do not skip the following chapters. You use energy every day and unless you remember to practise what you have just learnt you could easily fall by the wayside and only **Act** positive and perhaps **Believe** positive, but once you forget to **Cast** off negative energy you allow others to control you and your mind. When you practise all of your **Positive Energy ABC** you take control of your life and more importantly your mind.

CHAPTER NINE

Magnetic 'Cheese'

A Reminder of How Energy Works

Some people think that energy cannot be seen. But it can always be seen and felt. Once it has been felt, you can see it quite clearly, even if you have not noticed it before. Positive energy shines out and we are attracted to it. Negative energy is dull, we are repelled by it. Positive people smile, negative people frown. This is how we at first 'feel' energy, and then how we 'see' energy. People's emotions change with both energies.

Think of the energy around us as a magnet. When two negative magnetic energies are put together they fall apart. This is what happens when two people with negative energies meet. They cannot connect so cannot help each other and work together. They feel flat and don't have the energy to do anything for themselves, let alone together.

When two positive magnets are put together they will also not connect, yet two positive people will and do connect. This is because the energy around them feels electric and when their energies connect it creates a charge that feels electric and they 'spark' ideas and thoughts off each other.

We all have auras around our bodies. This is the energy we produce, and although most people cannot see auras, it is always felt. When we are positive about everything in our life we positively shine as our aura expands. It reaches out and touches those around us, and when they receive some of the positive energy they feel happier and thus more positive about everything in their lives.

This is why two positive people bounce when they meet. Their auras have expanded because it is filled with their love, hope, happiness and positive energy and when the two energies touch each other they bounce back as if charged with electricity. Anyone around them will feel this 'sparkling energy' and will want to stay near it.

Negative people fall apart when they meet because their auras have drawn nearer to their bodies. It has gone flat. The electric charge around them, so to speak, is not working as it should do. When something doesn't work it gets thrown out or rejected.

This is how negative people feel. They feel unworthy and unwanted; everything around them seems dull because they draw more negative people and situations into their lives. They find it very hard to accept and receive loving energy and emotion. Because they have received so much anger, pain and neglect in their life, it is all they want to give back, or know how to give back, because negative energy hurts and they want to give it back and hurt others too.

Negative energy and positive energy on the other hand sticks together. Why is this? If negative energy repels, why does it attract a positive energy and vice a versa?

There are two reasons. The first, because a positive energy is so attractive, the person with it laughs, smiles and sends out their love so that a negative person is drawn to it and wants to stick near this person. They want to feel some of this loving energy. It feels good; it is so different to the energy they normally receive. Positive people enjoy sharing their energy and so are happy to help jumpstart a negative person's flat energy by sending them some of their positive spark.

When you are around a lot of positive people the air around them feels light. The atmosphere is 'high'. It feels good to be near them.

The second reason is that negative energy is felt by all who receive it. Remember, **negative energy repels.** So, when negative people enter the room and send out this negative energy by moaning, groaning or even shouting; everyone whether positive or not, feels this energy as it sticks to them. It lowers the energy in the room. The atmosphere becomes thick and claustrophobic as it attaches itself to the positive energy that shines out and instantly flattens it.

Anyone receiving this energy will instinctively give the same energy back, unless they **Cast** it off. If they are being shouted at, they will start shouting. If a person is moaning or groaning, then they will find themselves joining in. The positive person will lose their 'sparkle' as the energy around them lowers.

However, if there are enough positive people in the room they will be able to share each other's positive energy and find it easier to **Cast** off any negative energy that this one person is trying to send out. And if they continue to send positive energy to the person who is shouting eventually the person will absorb some of the positive energy that is in the room and gradually start giving it back.

Positive people are attracted to each other because they know how good positive energy feels and they want to keep it. They don't want to receive any negative energy and feel flat.

If everyone reading this could bring more positive energy into their lives, by their thoughts and actions, then the air around us would feel positively wonderful.

All it takes to bring positive energy into your life is a smile. Smiles send out love, hope, positive energy, and a feeling of being wanted. Next time you see someone moaning or groaning, give them a smile. Let them feel how good that warm loving energy is. If they receive enough smiles they will become more positive about everything in their life and want to share it with others too.

'Cheese' is one of the words a photographer will use to help us to smile and light up the photograph he is taking.

So let us all say **'cheese'** and our smiles will raise the positive energy in our world, and make peace in our time a reality, and not just a dream.

CHEESE!

SMILE AND LET EVERYONE FEEL LOVED

CHAPTER TEN
Office Rage – How to Avoid It

Rage in any form is because a person is filled with negative energy from someone else giving them anger in one form or another and because it hurts so much they want to give it away as quickly as possible to another person, or persons.

Remember that negative energy repels and if you take their anger you will want to repel others by passing it on to them.

What do you do though if the person with rage is your boss or someone of equal importance? By screaming at you and taking control of your energy it makes them feel good because they think they are getting rid of their rage. Whereas in fact they could be just fuelling it and allowing it to spread further and not realizing it could come back to them tenfold.

Firstly, let's help you, the employee or person receiving this energy. What do you do? I have said that a smile is the quickest and easiest way to raise the positive energy, but in this instance it may only fuel their anger if you smile at them. You could be accused of insolence or not taking them seriously.

Negative energy hurts, and your brain as in that room full of smoke described in Office Two, starts to suffocate and you won't be able to think. You will start to panic and either say things you don't mean to them, or worse, believe their words that you are inadequate, an idiot, and second best.

If it is possible you need to find a way to get yourself out of that situation as quickly as possible. Apologize if necessary, but you need to get away from the energy as soon as possible.

Once away from this office you now have to **Cast** off the negative energy that you've been given. Don't allow yourself to sit there moaning about the person or telling others about the situation. This is what negative energy likes and how it infiltrates people's minds with smoke.

If you can, get outside and breathe fresh air and sit somewhere quiet, or better still find some happy people to be with and take their energy.

But, what if you can't and you have to sit in the same office as the person, or somewhere nearby?

There are many ways to deflect negative energy. I personally like to visualize a big pink bubble being sent to the person who is sending the rage. Whilst my mind is visualizing it floating towards them and filling them with pink loving positive energy I am not listening to what they are saying and so not allowing their energy to touch me. I am also allowing them to feel a different and nicer energy by giving them this pink bubble of love.

I then make sure that I send **myself** a pink bubble so that instead of dark negative energy touching me I can give myself some of this loving positive energy and by now my mind will be thinking clearer and should be able to think of something to say that will defuse the situation and as the perpetrator has also been sent a different energy they should hopefully now listen.

Pink bubbles are my way of dealing with negative situations, but you may be able to think of a different way. Count to ten. Bite your lip. Whatever way you have learnt to use in such circumstances and find it works, then use it, but always remember to stay in **CONTROL** of your own energy. Don't let them take it over, and most importantly of all, continue to **Cast** off their negative energy.

I use pink bubbles because I know that they work. Many times I have been standing in long queues, for example at the post office, and the people in front have been moaning at the long wait. I am sure you have been in this situation and watched as the person in front, or behind you moans and then the rest of the queue take this negative energy and start muttering and getting annoyed.

Think of the poor counter assistants. They are receiving and sitting in this energy all day. Negative energy suffocates and so they can't work as fast and they take longer to deal with each customer.

When this happens I turn and smile at the people behind me, giving them a positive lifting energy and to try and stop any negative energy spreading further than myself. I then smile at the person in front and then quickly send my famous pink bubbles to all in front, including the counter assistants and then visualize it going to those behind and then of course to myself.

I then start chatting to the person in front of me about something positive, even if it's just the weather, and yes if raining that is depressing, but make a joke of it. You will be very surprised at how quickly the energy changes in the room and how faster the queue moves.

Rage is the cause of many break ups whether at work, at home with your partner, or with friends. Whilst you are receiving this negative energy unless you do as above and get out of the situation then your mind is being suffocated and will be unable to think rationally.

Negative energy repels and you don't want it, so you intend to give it back tenfold. Harsh words are spoken and words that you don't mean to say. You just want to hurt the person as much as possible because they are hurting you. Sometimes harsh words can't be taken back and you lose something that you love or appreciate the most.

Learn to **Cast** off negative energy and diffuse the situation so that instead of both being in a room of explosive energy you are in a room filled with positive and fresh air so that at least you can listen to each other. People will always disagree with each other. It is human nature and it would be a very boring world if we all agreed with each other and had no opinion of our own. But positive people learn to listen and debate, not argue, fight and possibly start a war.

You've learnt how my **Positive ABC** works, so use it. Take control of your life with positive energy in everything that you do, think and say, and stop others trying to control you with their dark negative energies.

And, give yourself a pink bubble of love.

CHAPTER ELEVEN

How to Be Positively Beautiful

Spots! I bet you are either cringing straightway away because you have them and are wondering if this article is going to help you. Or, you don't have them so think this is not going to be for you.

Well, this book is for everyone regardless if you have spots or not. Nearly every one of you reading the book will have something you are not happy with, whether it is spots, freckles, the wrong size body, etc. The list is endless.

There won't be many people thinking there is nothing wrong with them and that they are beautiful. I hope though that a few of you are thinking this. It is not vain or wrong to think any of this. In fact it is positive.

Everyone is and can be beautiful. Beauty comes from the soul and the energy you give out. You will probably find that these people who think they are beautiful smile a lot and by smiling they are sending out a lot of positive energy to everyone around them.

They may well have spots or blemishes but you won't notice it because you will only see their smile and the glow that surrounds their body. When you are positive the energy around your body expands and other people feel it and to them you are a 'shining' example of beauty.

That's exactly what 'shining' means and how some people shine at everything they do and others don't. Yes, they may have made a lot more effort to 'shine' at something, but by making that effort, they've been positive about it.

Now we are going to deal with those spots and any other imperfections you think you may have. Please do carry on using any creams, potions, or medication you may have been recommended to help, (**Believe** in them), but also add a SMILE and some positive energy.

It doesn't cost anything and works very quickly because now instead of people staring at your spots etc, they are now looking at your lovely smile and the positive energy that shines out. Beauty is only skin deep, true beauty comes from within; from the soul. Someone who smiles and sends out positive loving energy has a beautiful soul and this shines out letting others see your true beauty, not those imperfections!

No negative thoughts such as, "she hasn't got a face full of spots or a blemish, so she doesn't know what it feels like." It doesn't matter what it is, just by thinking you are imperfect, you are sending out the message to everyone around you that you are. Your negative energy is affecting them and that is all they can see.

If, on the other hand you smile at people, then that is what they will see and the more you smile the more beautiful you become, because your soul opens up and your positive energy shines out and you start feeling good, and then everyone notices it.

Spots may still be there, but who is going to notice them if you smile and are shining with positive energy? Not me for one!

CHAPTER TWELVE

How to Mirror Your Thoughts

Mirror, mirror on the wall who is the fairest of us all? Every one who smiles at the mirror of course!

If everybody smiled at their mirror then peace in our time could become a reality and not just a dream. Every one of us would, metaphorically speaking, 'love our neighbour' and be less inclined to argue or fight, so ultimately less inclined to start that war. All of this from just smiling at your mirror!

The mirror echoes our thoughts. When we smile, it means we like what we see and others watching feel the warmth, love, hope and positive energy this smile sends out.

Your smile is your face to the world. Everyone who smiles raises the positive energy in the world a little higher. Everyone who frowns lowers it and the energy they send out makes all around feel sad, gloomy, lethargic and angry.

When someone is feeling angry and they shout at another person, that person instinctively gives the anger back, and then also takes it away with them and can spread it to others.

That's all it takes to start a war; one person shouting at another person, who then takes that energy away and gives it to others.

If, on the other hand, everyone raised the energy all around us by that lovely positive smile, the air would feel wonderful; we'd feel positively alive and so happy that when we encountered some of this negative energy we would **Cast** it off.

When you know how good positive energy feels you want to keep it in your life and won't allow negative energy to enter it.

A very good reason why you should smile at your mirror.

Once you've seen your face light up with that smile and felt how good it feels, you know then what others see and feel when they receive it. A smile always makes the receiver feel wanted. Next time you see someone frowning, or looking sad or gloomy, please give them a smile. Raise the energy around them so that they will want to smile and also keep that positive feeling it is giving them.

Now to the people reading this who are unable to smile at anyone, and most importantly of all to themselves. Your life feels so bad; all you are receiving is negative energy through one form or another. It may be through control, anger, pain, or even that you don't like how you look. You don't love yourself. When you don't love yourself, you can't love others.

So, first we have to learn to love ourselves, which is why we smile at the mirror. Just look at your smile, nothing else. Smile and see how lovely you look. See how it feels when you tell yourself that smile is just for you, because you deserve it, you are beautiful.

Now look in the mirror and frown and see and feel the difference. It makes you feel sad and tired and fills your mind with negative thoughts that depress you, whilst the smile lights up your face and like the mirror echoes your positive thoughts. You feel and look beautiful and that is all anyone looking at you will see.

It doesn't matter if you think you are overweight, too thin, have spots, or anything else you don't like about yourself, because when you smile that's all other people will see.

Smiles are beautiful. The person smiling will 'shine' with positive energy and the person receiving it will feel the warmth it is sending out and also think what a beautiful person you are.

With everyone smiling and bringing more positive energy into their lives and all around them, then everyone will become more confident. Nothing is impossible, in fact everything is possible.

So let us all mirror our thoughts and know that we can all help to foster world peace by smiling and letting everyone feel loved.

CHAPTER THIRTEEN

Revision for a Positive Mind, Body, and Spirit

The mind, the body and the spirit. They all contribute to make one person – **YOU**. How this person lives, breathes and reacts, is all down to how you use your mind, body, and spirit.

Start by being positive about everything in your life. Positive energy is the key word that links your mind, body, and spirit. When you are positive about something then your mind is active and happy and sends out the right emotions to all of your body. This makes you feel good, look good, and you know you are good, and of course your spirit is part of you, and a positive spirit will raise all the energy inside you.

It is all down to us how we use our mind, body, and spirit. Use it wisely and you'll feel good. Use it wrongly and feel negative about everything, then your whole life will be in a turmoil. Negativity doesn't just make you look and feel bad, but it also lowers the energy of everything and everyone around you. Just by looking gloomy, feeling angry, or saying you are having a bad day is enough. Everyone else will experience the same feelings and want to give the same energy back.

The lower the energy, the harder it is to feel positive about anything. If on the other hand you are happy, smile and are pleasant to people, they will notice it. They will feel good when they are in your company.

Your positive energy will bounce all around them and lift their spirit, and then of course once their spirits are lifted and they are receiving some of your positive energy they will want to keep it and continue to feel good about themselves. Once they feel good about themselves, their mind, body, and spirit lifts, and they too become positive.

Once the people around you are feeling positive about themselves, the energy returns to you and you continue to feel good. It is positively good to feel this energy and share it with people.

Too many people use their mind, body, and spirit wrongly. They hate themselves, their lives and the people around them. The people around them receiving this negative energy give it back and it continues to spread all around leaving too many mind, body and spirits in the wrong frame of mind and energy.

If you are feeling angry or negative about something, start by relaxing about it all. Try and change the energy within yourself. Make it a positive one instead. Do something silly, watch something funny, all it will take is one smile and your mind, body and spirit will start to respond.

Your positive energy will rise and if you carry on raising it by laughing, smiling and feeling good about everything, soon all negative thoughts will disappear. Your mind, body, and spirit will be positive.

Doesn't it feel good when you are positive something is going to happen? Why let that positive feeling disappear then? Keep on being positive about yourself and everything in your life, and it will remain in your mind, body, and spirit.

Once you have a positive mind, body, and spirit and keep it within yourself, then you start to share this feeling with others. Just by being with you they feel more positive and they spread it to someone else. If we all had a positive mind, body, and spirit all negative thoughts and energies would go. The universe would be a happier and better place to live and breathe in.

Negative energy suffocates people, their mind, body, and spirit slowly dies and they can't be bothered, or are unable to do anything. They just don't have the mind, body, or spirit to do it.

We are all responsible for our own mind, body, and spirit, so we should look after it wisely. Start with more positive thoughts, be positive that you will be well, that you will be prosperous and that you will succeed in everything that you set out to do. Create the right energy within yourself, and all this not only will, but is possible, but first you have to be positive about it.

Mind, body, and spirit. What energy sits inside yours?

CHAPTER FOURTEEN

How to Hook That Man (Or Woman) through Divine Intervention

Want to hook that man, or woman, of your dreams? Do you need some divine intervention? Well, read on because here it comes.

The first thing you need to do is get a pen and paper. No, you are not writing him, or her, a love letter! What you are going to do is describe the man or woman of your dreams down to the very last detail, and no I don't run a mail order catalogue that sells men or women!

You are going to order this person via the energy in the universe, or the law of attraction. Write down precisely what you want and desire in this man, or woman of your dreams, (anyone can do it). You need to describe them down to the very last detail; height, age, colour of eyes, hair, and personality, absolutely everything.

Don't leave anything out, because if you do then it's your fault if he or she is not the person of your dreams! Observe friends in happy relationships, see what you like about it and add it to your list. Remember to expect the best for yourself halfway is no good, as that is all you'll get!

However, one word of warning, please do remember to put the words 'available' and whether 'gay or heterosexual' wanted. Think what a disaster it would be if you meet the person of your dreams and they say, "Sorry, I'm married," or, "Sorry, I'm gay." Or in the case of a gay person, "Sorry, I'm heterosexual." You would be devastated wouldn't you?

Well, we've made the first step into divine intervention. We've asked for the person of our dreams and described them down to the last detail. Now put this letter somewhere safe and positively believe that they are out there. Don't say, or let anyone else say, "The person you've asked for doesn't exist, they are too perfect," because they DO exist. **Cast** off that negative thought.

You have asked for them, so positively **Believe** that they exist, and don't say, "Well, I've no hope of getting someone like that." That message tells the person who is waiting for you somewhere in the unknown that they do not exist and that person won't come your way.

It's called the law of attraction. By telling that person you want them and you know that they are out there and that you **Believe** they will come into your life, they **WILL** come into your life. If, on the other hand you don't positively **Believe** it will happen, then by the law of attraction, they can't come into your life because you don't really believe that they exist. Be POSITIVE about the person you want and **BELIEVE** that they will come to you.

The next stage of divine intervention is to start **Acting** positive about everything you do from feeling positive about yourself, to how good you look, to being positive with what you can and will achieve.

You will find that once you start acting positive then you will attract positive people your way and more doors will open, and behind one of them is the person of your dreams waiting for you.

So, get that pen and paper right now and start writing by using the divine intervention. The person of your dreams is out there and just waiting to be asked for!

DON'T DISAPPOINT THEM, OR YOURSELF!

CHAPTER FIFTEEN

The Positive Side to Being Gay

Strange title many of you will think. Especially if you've been living in the closet, or just decided to come out.

People either know you are gay or have just found out. Which ever of these it is, be positive about being gay. Why shouldn't you be gay, what's wrong with being gay? Have you got two heads, do you live in a different world to the rest of us? No, I don't think so.

Some heterosexual people on the other hand certainly do live in a different world, but they are the ones who are not very positive about anything, so, it's not just because you are gay that they may be prejudiced about you; no these people are negative about everything.

Having read this far you will see that I always tell everyone to love themselves, because that is the first step to positive energy. So, even if you are afraid of letting people know you are gay, please do love yourself. Once you love yourself you will see how easily it is for others to love you. You're positive side will shine out and attract others towards you who are not just gay but happy too!

If you have a partner don't be frightened of letting people know that you love them. Be positive about it. Let others see you have a partner. Love can come in many forms, but whatever way it appears it is always positive and should be shared.

I don't know if there is still any prejudice in the work place regarding being gay, but if there is then why is it there? Once people know you are gay, you are more relaxed and positive about yourself and it will show in your work and you will positively shine at it.

In an ideal world there would be no 'them and us' in any form, be it sexuality, colour or religion. We would all love each other. That day is still a long way off, but we can bring it closer by all being more positive about ourselves and life.

Just think of the positive energy that could be raised if we were all positive. It would feel wonderful. Everyone would feel less inclined to argue or fight with anyone and more inclined to start being friendly and loving each other.

So guys/gals you can start by doing your little bit right now. Be positive about being gay. I think gay is a lovely word. It means happy. Start being happy about being gay and letting everyone share it.

CHAPTER SIXTEEN

A Little Positive Energy to Be Shared Around the World

U.S.A. AND HOW TO POSITIVELY USE YOUR
I.N.D.E.P.E.N.D.E.N.C.E

Instantly you say the word you think of freedom. America, the land of the free. It is also the land of positive energy. Firstly, you aim for the top and secondly you are polite. Two traits that raise the positive energy around us. By aiming for the top, or to be the best, you are brimming with energy and it touches the person next to you. Their energy reaches out to the next person and so on and so on. Positive energy spreads and feels good.

Nothing is too much trouble for you. "Have a good day," those few words were said so many times when I last visited your country, but they were always said with a smile. Smiles always make the receiver feel good and instantly that person leaves feeling a little more positive about their day. Good manners are not only always accepted, but also very welcome. Far better than a rude, unhelpful person who sends out negative signals and you leave feeling angry, annoyed, and fed up.

Does any of this sound or feel familiar? I hope so, because positive energy is sadly lacking in our world and we need to raise it before it becomes so full of negativity that we all end up hating and fighting each other.

I'm sure many of you are saying, "Yes, it would be lovely to have peace and end all wars." So, let us start by all doing our little bit towards it. Just by raising the positive energy, more people will start liking each other and loving their neighbour (metaphorically of course). Less hate will be felt and so people will be less inclined to start a war.

Every one of you who just smiles at someone else has taken the first step to raising that energy and sending love and light around the world.

Positive energy shines out when you smile. Have you ever sat next to someone who is frowning or constantly moaning? You can't wait to get away! That's because they are sending negative energy out and it feels bad. We don't want that energy in our world. Just think how bad we would all feel if everyone frowned or moaned.

Everything a person says, feels, or shows, sends out energy. Whether it is positive or negative is up to that person. Energy can always be seen and felt!

Now you've read this far, think what message you are sending out. Positive, I hope. If not, why not? A smile costs nothing. It is free. Free to give and free to receive, but the cost to the universe is vast. It is the start to that positive seed that will spread and affect everyone.

Don't delay, start today with a smile on your face and start feeling more positive about yourself. Try giving that smile to yourself as well. You deserve it too and if you're feeling happy then you will want everyone around you to feel happy. Makes sense doesn't it?

Energy feels far better when it is a positive one rather than a negative one. So keep aiming for the top and being positive that you are the best and deserve the best and keep on being polite, especially by smiling.

Nations will join together if enough positive energy is sent out. They will feel how wonderful it is and be more inclined to listen to each other and may finally understand what 'independence' really means - the end of all wars and a land where they are free.

Campaigns play a big part of creating independence for America. So make those campaigns positive. Let us all feel that energy and hope, and most of all love that you send out.

Energies start wars, but energies can also end wars. Let's keep the energy high and make sure you all aim for the top and are positive about it and remember to smile and let everyone feel loved.

Have a nice day.

AUSTRALIA AND HOW THOSE X'S MAY HELP WORLD PEACE

X's mean so many different things. When you sign them at the end of your letters it is sending the receiver your warm loving thoughts and energy. If on the other hand you see them on your exam sheet, it sends you sad, negative thoughts.

But to many of you reading this article the first thing you may have thought of was of course that tin it appears on. To drink from this can you need to use your lips, the part of the body that can be used in so many positive ways. To smile, to speak, to kiss and of course to eat and drink with. It can also be used in many negative ways. To frown, to shout and control.

If everyone realized how very important the lips were and that by using them positively we could help world peace, then I am sure most of you would do so. Positive energy attracts, negative energy repels. With more positive energy around, people will be more inclined to 'love their neighbour' (metaphorically speaking of course) and less inclined to fight them. Peace in our time may become possible, rather than a dream.

Smiles send out love, happiness and hope to people; even someone you don't know. Just by giving them a little smile you brighten their day, even if only for a short time, but that may be enough for them to smile at someone else and start that smile spreading elsewhere.

If everyone smiled at each other it would create a Mexican wave of positive energy that would spread throughout the universe. When people are positive, everything becomes possible, and nothing becomes impossible. Positive people listen to others; they are more sensitive of race, creed, sexuality and politics. They still may not agree with what someone says, but instead of arguing with that person and taking away their negative energy and spreading it to other people, they will use their positive energy and listen and debate without getting angry and possibly fighting.

Anger creates negative energy, the air around becomes thick and suffocating, it becomes difficult to hear what is actually being said. Instead, because it repels, you instinctively wish to give it back by shouting.

That's all it takes to start a war. One person to shout at another person and the receiver takes that anger and negative energy away and spreads it to others who then spread it even further.

On the other hand all it takes to stop a war is one person. One person to smile and if enough smiles are sent out the air around us would feel positively wonderful.

Think of when you have been with people who were happy and smiling, the atmosphere felt wonderful, you wanted to stay in it, but when you did leave you took this positive energy away and shared it with others.

Now, think of when you have been in the company of people who were moaning, groaning or even arguing. I am sure you instinctively found yourself joining in and spreading more negative energy and when you left them you may not have realized it but you probably spread that negative energy to others.

Universal energy, it us the people on this planet who make it a positive or negative one to live in. Too much negative energy will cause more fights and ultimately those wars, but with more positive energy, people will listen and help stop those wars.

Let's make 'X' a positive sign and use our lips to bring world peace. So, start by smiling and raising the positive energy by helping everyone to feel loved.

Jill Divine X

ENGLAND – WHERE MY MEXICAN WAVE OF SMILES IS STILL RIPPLING

England - the land of hope and glory. We've learnt to smile through all weathers and all adversity. It's not easy being British when you're picnicking in June and the weather changes to hail and large hail stones pelt down and chill your cuppa. The British have an odd expression about 'keeping your upper lip stiff', in other words keep positive whatever the situation.

During the last two wars the people at the top had to believe that we would win and by being positive passed their energy on to the general public to help them through the bad times and keep them smiling.

The wars taught us many lessons; people rallied around and held street parties by sharing food rations. Couples still got married and despite the war had wonderful weddings with everyone finding ways to help make their day memorable. Cakes were made without eggs. Meat was scarce but pies were still made even though they were now filled with vegetables. Nothing was impossible, there was always a way to make things happen.

They had so little, but they learnt to be positive and find a way to make so much.

Today, we have so much and most importantly of all we are free to live our lives how we please and without the threat of being controlled by someone else.

Let's keep that wartime spirit going by being positive. Let's remove any negative energy that is around us by smiling and sharing it with others so that they can feel its happy energy and find a way to make things happen without arguing or fighting.

Let's love our neighbour (metaphorically speaking please. I don't want any law suits)!

CHAPTER SEVENTEEN
Positive Energy Alphabet©

Having learnt your **Positive Energy ABC**, then let's continue to the **Positive Energy Alphabet.** With this your world will open up and expand. You will achieve everything that you want to do in life.

Act positive, and then most importantly,

Believe positive, and then you will be able to

Cast off negativity.

Doesn't positive energy feel good? Once you've cast off negativity you can

Expect to succeed. So,

Feel how good that positive energy is.

Great isn't it?

Have faith and trust that it will work.

Instantly you believe positive, you will succeed.

Just listen to your thoughts and the energy you are sending out.

Kind,

Loving thoughts sends out positive energy, that

Makes others feel positive too.

Negative thoughts on the

Other hand

Produce negative results.

Quite the wrong sort of energy you want to live in.

Remember how good that positive energy feels, so

Start

Today with a positive thought, and everything that was previously

Unbalanced in your life

Vanishes and

Will now fade and

E**X**pire, because now you know how energy feels,

You will always want to live in a positive

Zone.

And all of this energy will come from just knowing your **Positive Energy ABC**

CHAPTER EIGHTEEN

Last Chapter

The last page before you all receive your diplomas. How well have you done with your **Positive Energy ABC?** I am **POSITIVE** that once you've read how you can see and feel both energies, and how life becomes so much easier with your **Positive Energy ABC,** that everyone of you reading this book will now continue to use it.

You can now see that all it takes to start that war is one person:-

ONE PERSON TO SHOUT AT ANOTHER PERSON. THE PERSON RECEIVING THAT NEGATIVE ENERGY IS REPELLED, SO TAKES THAT ENERGY AWAY WITH THEM, AND SPREADS IT TO OTHERS.

Angry people have no control of their thoughts or words and arguments can spiral out of control and explode. If you imagine anger as a small pile of lit dynamite that grows as it spreads to others sharing this anger then it is easy to see the end result.

BANG! An almighty explosion as they come together.

A WAR HAS STARTED!

But remember, all it takes to stop that war is one person. One person with positive energy sharing their lovely positive smile. With more positive people in the world, they will be more sensitive to race, creed, sexuality, and politics, because positive people **LISTEN.** They may not still agree, but instead of an explosive and negative argument, they will listen and debate the subject.

Positive people will also find a way to solve all solutions. Because their mind is full of that fresh clean positive air, it is able to think clearly of a way around everything. Whereas negative people are suffocated with that thick black negative energy where nothing they think, or say, makes sense. They are unable to think rationally and so will never solve any solutions.

If you have understood all of this, then you **DESERVE** this diploma, because you have **SUCCEEDED** in:-

Acting positively, and most importantly of all

Believing positively. So you have

Cast off all negativity.

POSITIVE ENERGY ABC DIPLOMA

I hereby confirm that the following person has not only learnt and understood their **Positive Energy ABC,** but continues to keep it in their lives in everything they do and say. The world is now their oyster, because having learnt their basic **Positive Energy ABC,** they have continued positively on to read and understand their **Positive Energy Alphabet.**

Now:-

EVERYTHING IN THEIR LIFE BECOMES POSSIBLE

AND NOTHING BECOMES IMPOSSIBLE

CONGRATULATIONS!

NAME: (please print)

....

POSITIVELY SIGNED AND WITNESSED BY

Jill Divine

....

JILL DIVINE

All of Jill Divine's books can be seen on her website:-

www.divinelady.co.uk

Over the next few pages are sample chapters of a few of them. If you wish to read more you can purchase them on www.amazon.co.uk www.amazon.com and www.lulu.com

ANJOY – GOD'S GIFTS
ISBN: 1-4137-6465-7 (Science Fiction)
Published by PublishAmerica

Chapter 4
GOD'S GIFTS

Viola sat in front of the hologram of her beloved daughter, Anjoy. She was now twelve years old and very beautiful. Her long blonde hair shone in the light and Viola imagined what it would be like to brush it every night. Tears formed in her eyes as she realized she would never see her again after today. Why was Zut destroying the shrine? Didn't he realize the comfort it gave her and the twenty four other parents whose babies had been stillborn? She put her hand through the hologram and tried to feel Anjoy. Oh, if only she could touch her, stroke her face, kiss her, anything, even if it was only for a minute.

Her mind wandered back to Anjoy's birth twelve years ago. It was unheard of to lose a baby. Everything was followed meticulously. Women or men were not allowed to get pregnant before the age of fifty because they weren't considered mature enough to handle it before then. Plus from the ages twenty five to fifty everybody had to serve in the Planet Force. Up until then their brains were energized with information every day for sixty wixons. By the time they were twenty five they knew everything anyone could possibly ever want to know.

She was very proud when she was chosen to provide the main gene to create their first child. The pregnancy had been scanned and accelerated daily for the normal nine days and as usual there were no problems. It was only when they used the introducing wire that introduced the baby to the Transfer Room, where they inserted the wires needed to receive all the knowledge obtained from cerebrumadrome, that they realized she was dead. Pandemonium had followed in the Transfer Room. They had never known it happen before, but then it happened to twenty four other people.

Finally, when answers were demanded from those people that had been chosen next to create life, they found a minute fault in the acceleration process which only occurred in every tenth baby. It was accelerating the heart growth so fast that it aged it to two hundred and fifty years, meaning the heart was dead before the baby was even born.

She remembered the aftermath of their daughter's death. The wizend told them it was God punishing them for not believing in him and not being registered. Viola had even attended a few secret Faith meetings and in her distress was starting to believe her. Then they had a personal visit from their Leader who told them that was utter nonsense. God didn't exist. They asked if they could register as partners earlier than the normal age of seventy five. They didn't tell their Leader, but hoped this would appease God and that he would let them keep their next child. Their Leader wouldn't hear of it. Far too young he'd said. Once their first child started Planet Force that would be early enough. They only had twenty five years to wait so why were they being so impatient?

Viola wiped the tears away that were running down her face and prepared to switch the hologram off. She only had fifteen wixes of her visiting time left anyhow and she wanted to look at her daughter's smiling face without it being blurred by the tears. She wished Odraine had come with her to say goodbye, but he had said he couldn't bear it, knowing that when they switched off the Hologram Shrine today, that would be it. No more Anjoy.

They had never experienced the emotion of death before because it was accepted that everyone died at two hundred and fifty years. The night before the wizend went to the Farewell Room to die and their remains evaporated, everyone went to the Galiquer and had so many galiquons they could barely remember what the wizend looked like when they surfaced in the morning. Illness and accidents did not exist on Planet Tirleen. They had seen pictures of such things on their lens at cerebrumadrome from a thousand years ago, but now in the year 3030 transport was safe and no one became ill.

She wiped her face again as more tears poured down as she prepared to switch the hologram off. She blinked as she looked at Anjoy. Her mind must be playing tricks with her; she could have sworn that her daughter had waved at her. She smiled at Anjoy and waved back, realizing that Zut had probably programmed it into the hologram as a farewell present for them.

With a very heavy heart Viola switched the hologram off as the light came on to signal the end of visiting. She didn't want the Guardians doing it for her which they would do if she didn't obey Zut's orders and do it herself. The hologram of Anjoy faded and the tube went blank. Viola closed her eyes. She couldn't bear to see her daughter disappear. She was aware of some of the other parents screaming, but she was going to try and remain composed. Emotion was frowned on by Zut and she didn't want to be in trouble.

She wiped her face yet again so that she could see clearly to leave the Hologram Shrine and then bravely opened her eyes, preparing herself to look at the blank tube. The screaming in her ears echoed and she realized it was coming from her throat. Stood in front of the tube was her beloved daughter Anjoy, she was smiling at her and SHE WAS ALIVE!

THE BEARS
ISBN: 1-42410307X (Science Fiction)
Published by PublishAmerica

CHAPTER 3
PLANET KIRLIANUS – YEAR UNKNOWN

The line for the Energy Chamber was getting longer and longer and the Kirlianons at the end of the queue were getting impatient and very frantic. The green gunge dripping out of their hands was now spreading to their arms and they only had thirty minutes to get into the chamber to renew their energy aura before they died. This was a daily routine for them and normally it was not a problem, but recently the chamber had got low on energy and was taking longer and longer to renew their aura.

Those waiting in the queue watched their aura getting darker then blacker and prayed they would reach the chamber in time to be energized and come out with the violet aura they normally had. Today it seemed to be taking forever which was bad luck for the last four waiting in the queue, as their thirty minutes were now up. They screamed in terror as they watched the green gunge spread all over their body until they ended up as a green mess on the floor, then turned to dust and they completely disappeared.

Pandemonium now ensued as everyone pushed each other as they tried to reach the chamber. Aurulus and Rubicon, members of the Communication Chamber who helped rule the planet, decided that this was one of those occasions to use their rank to its full advantage. Creatus Chakrus was the ruler of the planet, but Aurulus was second and Rubicon third in command of the planet, so they felt quite justified in pushing the others out of the way. If they died who would have their knowledge and intelligence to take over their positions?

"Out of my way, out of my way," screamed Aurulus, breathing a sigh of relief as he reached the front of the chamber.

He got ready to jump in as Pyren came out, but just stopped himself in time. Aurulus shook with fear as he watched Pyren look at his hands in horror, wondering where the spiritual violet aura was that he should have after being energized. Pyren looked at the rest of his aura and his screams echoed around the room as it joined the rest of the Kirlianons who were now in a total panic. Pyren's aura was DARK BROWN! He'd been earthed, and not only that it was full of rips and holes. Something was very wrong with the Energy Chamber!

Aurulus looked at Rubicon, but Rubicon shook his head. He wasn't going in next. Aurulus was next in command, it was his place to test the chamber and see if it was working properly now. Aurulus hesitated. He knew he had to be energized but he didn't want to come out like Pyren. He could hear Pyren screaming at the operators asking what they'd done wrong, and watched Phenora and Emion check the control panel and shake their heads at him.

"There's nothing wrong with the control panel, you can go in now, Aurulus," said Phenora, and at the same time whispering to Emion, "The chamber must be getting weaker."

The screaming died down as the others watched and waited for Aurulus to go in. If he came out with a violet aura they'd be OK to follow. Perhaps it was just a temporary blip and Pyren was just the unlucky one? Aurulus looked at the chamber as he listened to Pyren's quiet sobbing, and decided that next in command or not, he wasn't going to risk it. Telepathically he asked Creatus Chakrus to come immediately to the Energy Chamber as there was a problem.

Creatus Chakrus was in the Communication Chamber looking around the planets and galaxies on a giant screen, occasionally stopping to focus on a particular one. He sighed when he received the message. *Now what was wrong,* he thought? He was fed up with the complaints about the chamber not energising their auras properly. So what if a few of them had rips and holes in them, at least they were still violet. He too was feeling a little irritated, but what could he do? He was trying to work on the problem at the moment, but as of yet had found nothing that could help them.

He flew into the Energy Chamber, where once again pandemonium ensued. More Kirlianons were slowly dissolving whilst the rest were screaming and panicking not knowing what to do, but too scared to enter the chamber.

"Quiet!" screamed Creatus Chakrus as he stood in the middle of the room. The room was immediately silent and everyone turned and bowed to their leader. "Why is the chamber empty?" he asked the operators.

Before they could speak, Aurulus pointed to Pyren. "The machine isn't working properly. I don't think it's safe to enter."

"Of course it is," said Creatus Chakrus, "just a temporary blip that's all. You're a member of the chamber, set an example, Aurulus, and go in first." He pushed Aurulus into the chamber and told the operators to start the machine working. Fifteen seconds later Aurulus came out and looked very relieved to find his aura bright violet. "I told you it was just a blip," said Creatus Chakrus, "now keep moving before you all expire, and don't bother me again unless it's really urgent."

With a sigh of relief the other Kirlianons started going into the chamber again. Unaware that Creatus had telepathically called the Crimsonites to the Energy Chamber Room.

The door opened and there was a rumbling as six enormous aliens with a vivid red aura and wearing black leather robes marched in. The Crimsonites guarded Kirlianus in exchange for a protection ring around their planet, D4-Crims. Normally the Kirlianons, being such a spiritual race, were unable to harm anyone, so the Crimsonites dealt with any unwanted visitors.

Today however Creatus Chakrus didn't feel very spiritual, in fact he felt down right irritated and destructive. He knew he had a few rips and holes in his aura and was hoping his next session in the chamber would repair them, but unfortunately for Pyren he'd chosen the wrong day to be the first person to come out with the wrong coloured aura!

Creatus Chakrus pointed to Pyren, as he spoke to Destructus Dargon, the leader of the Crimsonites. "Put this man in the Negatron Chamber and stay here and do the same to any others who come out of the energy chamber without a violet aura, we can't waste precious energy putting them back in our machine."

Pyren was dragged screaming into the Negatron Chamber by Destructus Dargon. The Negatron was normally only for use on any aliens who invaded their planet and had never been used on the Kirlianons before! It was the reverse of the Energy Chamber and instead of renewing their aura, slowly and painfully dissolved it. The unfortunate occupant felt like it was being torn from their body in pieces, then all the cells in the body spontaneously combusted and the person exploded. It was an agonising death!

Rubil laughed as he operated the Negatron. Pyren was screaming in agony as his aura was slowly torn into pieces, he had never experienced such pain before, and was clawing the glass door trying to get out. Blood was dripping down the glass as his body started breaking down, then there was a BANG, and thankfully for Pyren, he spontaneously exploded, death releasing him from the horrible ordeal!

Those waiting in the queue for the Energy Chamber looked on in horror; it could be them if the machine went wrong on their turn. "Please, please, let us come out violet," they all silently prayed. Terror now reigned in the room as Creatus flew out leaving them alone with the Crimsonites.

The Energy Chamber worked well for a while, and then fifteen in a row came out of it with a brown aura. Each one was led away screaming by the Crimsonites and pushed into the Negatron Chamber one at a time. Those being held prisoner suffering even more as they watched their friends agonising deaths, and wished they could will their body to die before they went into the Negatron Chamber. The Kirlianons waiting for the Energy Chamber watched with dread. The presence of the Crimsonites was very unsettling. Now instead of shouting and pushing, everyone was very quiet.

Aurulus and Rubicon stayed and watched their friends agonising deaths. They felt as members of the Communication Chamber it was their responsibility to make sure the Crimsonites didn't bend the rules. They didn't trust Destructus Dargon one bit, they had a feeling he was trying to find a way to take over their planet, and now their leader had just given him the fuel he needed by putting people of his own planet in the Negatron. That was meant to be used only for their enemies. Not them!

They finally left when they were satisfied the chamber was once again working normally and energising everyone with their violet aura. Aurulus telepathically commanded Phenora and Emion to summon him straight away if Destructus Dargon started putting others in the Negatron. He wished he could find a way to stop anyone going in there, but if he went over Creatus's head then he was angry enough to shove him in there too!

POETRY EMOTION

ISBN: 978-1-4452-3529-5

Poetry that will help to inspire and put you in touch with your own emotions whether you are a lover of poetry or not.

Here are a few poems from the book.

A positive Poem:

THE NEW ABC

Many of us do **Act** positive I am pleased to say.

But then a negative thought will come our way.

That stops us **Believing** in what we're planning to do.

And we no longer have the confidence to follow it through.

So, **Cast** off that thought, don't let it get in your way,

For just one negative thought can spoil your whole day.

Believe in yourself; positively **Believe** in what you're planning to do

Believe you WILL succeed and that all your dreams WILL come true.

But this will only happen if you practice your new **ABC**

Act positive, **Believe** positive and **Cast** off any negativity.

Remember your thoughts can change the whole outcome

A Painful poem:

ANGER

Anger's so painful you want to give it away

You send it to others hoping that's where it will stay.

But anger's like a lit fuse and once it is shared

Harsh words are spoken as tempers become flared.

And if it's not stopped and those lit fuses put out

Fighting will follow, of that there's no doubt

And war will come next as all those tempers EXPLODE

Giving their pain to others as their anger they offload.

An Angelic Poem

TRUE LOVE

The angel gazed down at the babe in her arms.

His innocence was beautiful and one of his charms.

She'd waited so patiently having heard his prayer

To bring him to safety and her tender care.

The babe sighed softly, he was safe at last.

All his pain and suffering were now in the past.

No longer alone suffering neglect from his mother.

Or feeling the pain dished out by her lover.

The angel's heart opened and her love poured out.

This was much better than a thump or a shout.

The angel caressed him and her love it did show.

Because on the babe's face was a positive glow.

He knew this was true love, this didn't smart.

So different to the feeling of his mother's heart.

His mother had smothered him, but not with her love.

The angel had rescued him and shown him true love.